How To Make A

BABY GIRL

or

BABY BOY

Choose the Sex of Your Child
In Plain and Simple Language

Mark Moore, MD and Lisa Moore, RN

Illustrated by Jeff Parker

Second Edition

WASHINGTON PUBLISHERS

www.washingtonpublishers.com

How To Make A
BABY GIRL or BABY BOY–
Choose the Sex of Your Child
In Plain and Simple Language

Text Copyright © 2005 Mark Moore, MD, Lisa Moore, RN
Illustrations Copyright © 2005 Mark Moore, MD, Lisa Moore, RN
Published by Washington Publishers SAN: 2542366

Washington Publishers
P.O. Box 12517
Tallahassee, Florida   32317
(850) 222-2222

Moore, MD, Mark; Moore, RN, Lisa
How To Make A BABY GIRL OR BABY BOY–
Choose the Sex of Your Child
In Plain and Simple Language
ISBN   0-9715721-2-7

Summary: An easy-to-read handbook which details natural methods
that may make it more likely to conceive either a baby girl or baby boy.

1. Pregnancy and Childbirth
2. Reproductive Health
3. Gender Preselection
4. Preconception Family Planning
5. Parenting

Edited, printed and published in the USA
First Edition: January 2002
Second Edition: January 2005

Volume discounts available to physicians' offices.

TABLE OF CONTENTS

FORETHOUGHT

There is nothing more wondrous than to observe the birth of a child...except, maybe, to watch her or him grow up.

Instructions for use:

1.   To fully understand the principles of this book, we encourage you to read each page in its entirety.

2.   Repeat instruction #1.

INTRODUCTION

This book is written in simple language to help future parents apply methods to make it more likely to have either a baby girl or boy. Normally it's approximately a 50-50 chance, However, when closely followed, the techniques outlined in this book can improve those odds to as high as 80-20 in your favor.

The most famous person who tried to prearrange the sex of his children was King Henry VIII. After reading this, you'll agree he could have satisfied his desire for male heirs simply by monitoring his bedchamber activities!

THE MAN

The man has TESTES (testicles) which make and store the SPERM.

These testes live in the SCROTUM (external scrotal sac) to control the proper temperature for sperm production, which is slightly cooler than the body's normal temperature of 98.6 degrees Fahrenheit.

TESTOSTERONE is a male hormone made by the testes, which assists in the production and growth of the sperm.

The SPERM COUNT is the concentration of sperm cells in ejaculate, which parallels male fertility. During sex, the man ejaculates about 1/8 ounce of semen, containing approximately 200–300 million sperm. Frequent intercourse or oral sex will lower the volume of ejaculate and it can take 24 hours to 48 hours to return to normal levels.

THE SPERM

The man produces two types of sperm:
X-SPERM and Y-SPERM. During conception,
only one single sperm cell unites with the woman's
egg and determines the baby's gender.
(BABY GIRL when the X-Sperm unites with the egg
or BABY BOY when the Y-Sperm unites with the egg)

The sperm have different characteristics as described
below:

X-SPERM traits:
oval heads, move slower, live longer,
much stronger, far fewer X-Sperm than Y-Sperm

Y-SPERM traits:
round heads, move faster, die faster, more fragile,
many more Y-sperm than X-sperm

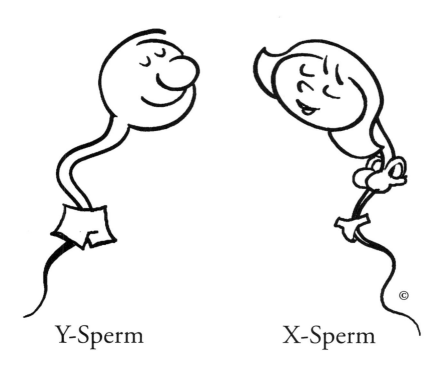

Y-Sperm   X-Sperm

THE WOMAN

The woman has two OVARIES and a UTERUS (womb). The EGG grows in either of the ovaries under the influence of female hormones such as estrogen.

Once a month on the OVULATION DATE, an egg bursts out from an ovary and travels down the FALLOPIAN TUBES into the uterus. CONCEPTION occurs if it happens to unite with the sperm there, and the egg implants itself as a new entity called a ZYGOTE. This represents the start of an extraordinary process—the development of your future baby.

Note: When a female reaches orgasm, her body produces an emission of alkaline fluids, which can help the Y-Sperm if it occurs *before* the male ejaculation.

THE EGG

The woman produces only one type of EGG—the X-Egg. Sometimes multiple eggs burst out, and if each one becomes fertilized by the sperm, multiple births such as twins or triplets can result. In these cases, each fertilized egg will create individually unique *fraternal* siblings. Sometimes one fertilized egg splits once or more, creating exact duplicate babies, known as *identical* twins or triplets.

THE CYCLE

The female monthly CYCLE is extremely important in determining the OVULATION DATE. Typically, the average cycle is 28 days, although normal variation and irregularity sometimes occur— even in the same female. Under the influence of female hormones such as estrogen, the lining of the uterus grows to prepare for the possibility of egg fertilization. Should this not occur during a cycle, the uterine lining disintegrates and discharges as menstrual flow.

- Day 1 is the first day of bleeding
- Bleeding usually lasts from Day 1 through Day 5
- Day 14 is the ovulation date in a consistent 28-day cycle, but this can vary

Ideally, the female should track her BASAL BODY TEMPERATURE for two months on a paper graph. It's best to do this every morning before getting out of bed (details on page 20).

Ovulation corresponds to a day on the graph when the woman's body temperature falls slightly and then suddenly rises by at least a degree Fahrenheit. Some women may feel an abdominal "tingle" around the time when the egg "bursts" out, corresponding to a surge in hormone levels. Specific ovulation kits, which can measure these hormone peaks, are available in your local pharmacy and can be quite accurate.

CONCEPTION

There are three players:
1. Egg (X)
2. Sperm (X)
3. Sperm (Y)

With two possible results:
1. X-egg and X-sperm make XX (baby girl)
2. X-egg and Y-sperm make XY (baby boy)

TRYING FOR A BABY GIRL

You want the X-SPERM to be more plentiful in this case. Determine the OVULATION DATE. Because the X-Sperm live longer, you should have sexual intercourse 3 days BEFORE your calculated OVULATION DATE. This means that mostly X-Sperm will survive to fertilize the egg 3 days later.

Follow steps one through eight as outlined on the next page. Acidic vinegar douche and dietary influences (pg 24).

INCREASE YOUR CHANCES OF HAVING A
BABY GIRL:

For discussion purposes, let's use an ovulation date of Day 14.

1. In order to lower the sperm count, have *frequent* intercourse (or other activities) on Days 5 through 8 (shaded days on graph below). This means mostly X-Sperm will prevail.
2. On Days 9,10 and 11, have *daily* intercourse using the methods described below.
3. The sexual position should be face-to-face.
4. Keep foreplay to a minimum.
5. During the man's climax, he should pull back and deposit shallow.
6. Avoid artificial lubricants during sex.
7. You may have sex on Days 12 through 16, but you *must* use condoms.
8. The mini-calendar below can be used as a guide.

Sun	Mon	Tue	Wed	Thur	Fri	Sat
	FREQUENT SEX TO LOWER SPERM COUNT				YES!	YES! 1
YES! 2	PS 3	PS 4	OD PS DAY 14	PS	PS	

YES! = Have sex on these days using the methods described on this page.
OD = Ovulation Date
PS = "Protected Sex" – Must use condoms with sexual intercourse on these days.

-17-

TRYING FOR A BABY BOY

You want the Y-SPERM to be more plentiful and make its way to the EGG easier and faster. That's why you must first determine your OVULATION DATE, and avoid sexual intercourse and activity at certain times to build up the sperm count.

Follow steps one through ten as outlined on the next page. Alkaline douche and dietary influences (pg. 10 and 24).

INCREASE YOUR CHANCES OF HAVING A
BABY BOY:

1. No intercourse (or anything else!) for 3 to 4 days before the calculated OVULATION DATE. This will help INCREASE the SPERM COUNT.
2. No hot tubs, baths or briefs for the man for the week prior to the ovulation date.
3. Have intercourse ONE TIME ONLY on the OVULATION DATE, and use condoms for any sex during the next 2 to 3 days.
4. Ideally, the woman should reach orgasm before the man.
5. Enjoy long foreplay and sexual excitement to maximize sperm emission.
6. The male should enter the female from behind ("doggie-style")
7. At climax, the man should deposit deeply.
8. The man should drink coffee or caffeinated soda 2 hours before sex, which can increase sperm counts.
9. After sex, sperm retention is improved if the female lies still for 20 minutes or longer.
10. Avoid artificial lubricants during sex.

OVULATION CHART

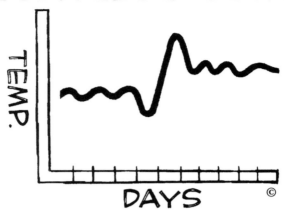

1. Use a specific Basal Body Temperature thermometer available in your local pharmacy. It includes a blank chart for daily recording.
2. Measure temperature at the same time each morning before arising, and record for 2 months.
3. The OVULATION DATE (OD) occurs when there is a slight temperature drop followed by a sudden rise in temperature (a degree or more). See sample chart above.
4. Most commonly, the ovulation date will be 14 days prior to the beginning of your next cycle. For example: 28-Day cycle, OD is Day 14 (28-14=14); on a 34-Day cycle, OD is Day 20 (34-14=20).
5. Also note there is an increase in the amount and slipperiness of vaginal mucus at ovulation date.

GET PREGNANT, FAST!

If you want to get pregnant fast, (and are not concerned whether you'll have a girl or boy):

A. Female to determine her ovulation date (p. 20).

B. Have frequent sex (at least daily) starting on the morning of your predicted ovulation date and continuing for 3 days.

C. Turn to page 19 and follow steps 1, 2, 4, 5, 6, 7, 8, 9 and 10. (Do not use Step 3).

D. Repeat as necessary.

PREGNANCY POINTERS

Choose healthy foods; take your vitamins and folic acid.
Avoid alcohol, cigarettes, drugs and stress.
See your obstetrician or midwife regularly.
Read another good book on pregnancy.
Avoid gaining too much weight.

Breast feed for 6 months—it's good for baby and mama; then consider using a high-quality formula (in place of whole milk) within their diet until sixteen to eighteen months. If you have a video camera, tape 60 seconds of video and audio each week, beginning with the last 3 months of pregnancy and continuing on for several years. Watch this video journal every year on your child's birthday. Make the most of the early years because your little ones will grow up fast.

EITHER WAY, IT SHOULD BE FUN TRYING

- Strengthening your relationship
- Trying new things
- Having more sex
- Discussing stuff

So "go forth and multiply," and remember, each child is a gift to his or her family and the world no matter what the gender.

MISCELLANEOUS

WARNING! Before using any douche (which can alter vaginal secretions) or changing your diet, you must *CONSULT YOUR OB/GYN, PHYSICIAN OR MIDWIFE.*

Acidic/vinegar douche prior to sex – favors baby girl
Add 2 tablespoonfuls of vinegar to a quart of sterilized water (boiled then cooled to room temp before use), and mix in sterilized douche bottle. Make within 2 hours of use.

Alkaline douche prior to sex – favors baby boy
Add 2 tablespoonfuls of baking soda to 1 cup of sterilized water (boiled then cooled to room temp before use), and mix in sterilized douche bottle. Make within 2 hours of use.

Mother-to-be's diet high in calcium and magnesium, like milk, cheese, cereals and beans for the month before trying, may favor a Baby Girl.

Mother-to-be's diet high in sodium and potassium, including vegetables, meats, fish and bananas for the month before trying, may favor a Baby Boy.

*Dietary factors have less influence on the baby's gender than other factors described in this book. A good general rule is to eat a healthy diet during the time you are *trying* to get pregnant and continue this during your entire pregnancy.

DISCLAIMER

The authors and publisher specifically disclaim any responsibility or any liability for loss or risk, personal or otherwise, which is incurred directly or indirectly from the use and application of any of the contents within this book. While simplified for our readers into an easy-to-read text, there is an enormous variety of conclusions and opinions within this subject matter. We assume no liability for errors, omissions or differences of opinion. Its authors are not engaged in rendering professional services or medical advice in the context of this book.

If you are having difficulty getting pregnant, then you should *NOT* do anything that might lower sperm counts as it could also lessen your chances of becoming pregnant, too. Sperm counts can be temporarily lowered when using the techniques of "trying for a baby girl." If you have irregular monthly cycles, it may be difficult to fulfill the details described in "trying for a baby girl" as your ovulation date may occur earlier than expected.

As always, consult your obstetrician, physician or midwife.

PREGNANCY MYTHS

If the baby's heartrate is FAST, it's a girl;
   if SLOW, it's a boy.

If the mother craves SWEETS, it's a girl;
   mother craves SOUR, it's a boy.

If the mother carries HIGH, it's a girl;
   carries LOW, a boy.

If the mother is SLEEPY, it will be a girl;
   ENERGETIC mom, a boy.

If the baby kicks LOW in the belly, it's a girl;
   if kicks HIGH in the ribs, a boy.

If mother likes to sleep on her RIGHT side, a girl;
   mother sleeps on the LEFT side, a boy.

If grandma has COLORED hair, it will be a girl;
   if she has GREY hair, it will be a boy.

If mother carries SIDEWAYS, it will be a girl;
   if carries in FRONT, it will be a boy.

STEP-BY-STEP INSTRUCTIONS

1. Female to determine her ovulation date. The more regular a woman's cycle, the easier and more accurate it will be. (Refer to page twenty.)

2. Use a blank calendar to mark the letters "OD-14" on the predicted ovulation date for the month you wish to begin trying (see example below).

3. Number the days back to Day 5 and forward to Day 16.

4. Review this book with special attention to pages sixteen through twenty.

JAN. 2005

"LISA C"

SUN	MON	TUES	WED	THUR	FRI	SAT
				1		
2	3	4	5	6	7	8
9	10	11	12	13	14 **DAY 5**	15 **DAY 6**
16 **DAY 7**	17 **DAY 8**	18 **DAY 9**	19 **DAY 10**	20 **DAY 11**	21 **DAY 12**	22 **DAY 13**
23 **OD 14**	24 **DAY 15**	25 **DAY 16**	26	27	28	29
30	31					

In this example, Lisa C's predicted ovulation date for the next month is Sunday, January 23 (designate as OD 14). Number the days back to Day 5 (January 14th) and forward to Day 16 (January 25th). If you still have any questions, your OB/GYN or midwife can assist.

AFTERWORD

This book is most effective when reviewed several times, preferably with your spouse or partner.

Once you've made the decision to bring a baby into your world, you've embraced life in an entirely new light. While this book was designed to help you make the most of methods that could possibly determine your baby's gender, each infant represents a gift—whether a girl or boy.

Nothing can compare to the miracle of life—the cry of your newborn drawing the first breath or the innocence of this new baby cradled in your arms.

That's why it is important to read everything you can about your pregnancy and become familiar with the changes that occur in your body and the expectations of future parenthood. Be generous with your time and love.

For a list of resources and suggested reading, please visit us at www.washingtonpublishers.com

DEDICATIONS

Dedicated to our beautiful children, our moms and dads, brothers and sisters, aunts and grannies, friends near and far, friends old and new, our teachers, instructors and mentors, the surgeons and staff we have worked with, those who have cared for us, counselors that have guided us, and of course, to the future mothers of our world's children.

A special thanks to those who have helped make this book possible, particularly Jeff and Pat for your wonderful illustrations and insight.

ABOUT THE AUTHORS

Mark Moore, MD, is a husband, father, writer, inventor and teacher. He is a Diplomate of the American Board of Anesthesiology and board-certified in pain management, with subspecialties in obstetric and pediatric anesthesia.

Lisa Moore, RN, his wife, is a mother and a pediatric nurse. Together they have a girl, a boy, a dog and a bird.

Fill our this page to create your baby's first keepsake.

IF YOU ARE A BABY GIRL, YOUR NAME MIGHT BE:

First   Middle

1. _____   1. _____

2. _____   2. _____

3. _____   3. _____

4. _____   4. _____

5. _____   5. _____

We'll call you by _____ or _____ .

IF YOU ARE A BABY BOY, YOUR NAME MIGHT BE:

First   Middle

1. _____   1. _____

2. _____   2. _____

3. _____   3. _____

4. _____   4. _____

5. _____   5. _____

We'll call you by _____ or _____ .